LESSONS LEARNED

—— from ——

My Rescue Dog

By
Mollie Singh

It's A Hat, LLC

LESSONS LEARNED FROM MY RESCUE DOG
Copyright © 2018 Maulik Singh. All rights reserved
www.molliesingh.com

Book Cover design and Interior Layout by CirceCorp Design

First Edition, 2018

ISBN : 978-1-7328921-0-1

To Glenn - I am me because we are we.

TABLE OF CONTENTS

Natty Picked Me

I n January 1993, I adopted a purebred papillon. She was beautiful. She was a sweet, happy soul and a puppy who became everyone's sweetheart. I named her Ashley. When I got Ashley, she had a cough. They called it kennel cough, but that cough never went away. And to boot, she was not growing at a rate that would have been considered normal. We found out that she was really sick. I was so in love with this creature, there wasn't anything I wouldn't do for her. There wasn't anything I wouldn't risk for her. She'd go in for observation, treatment, and even surgery. So, in January 1994, when the doctors told me that the chance that the surgery would work to help her was less than 40%, I truly believed my heroic financial efforts and my love for her would be enough.

But her little five-pound body just could not survive it. She did come home after surgery, but just whimpered endlessly when she was sleeping with me. I just kept petting her and telling her that I loved her. And then she stopped breathing. And it seemed like instantly, her body was stiff. I was devastated. This completely rocked my world. I couldn't sleep, I couldn't eat, I couldn't keep a thought in my head. The ast to return was my sleep. As an added bonus, I was suddenly allergic to any and all dogs and cats. It was awful. I had had cats as a child, and I absolutely love dogs… but suddenly I was horribly allergic to them all. I knew it was psychosomatic, but there was little I was able to do about it. No medication worked.

Then in 2004, I met and married a man who had a cat. As it turned out, as long as this cat did not come on the bed, I could co-exist in the same house. That cat was a loner and curmudgeon for sure, so staying out each other's way was a benefit to us both. I fed him and let him in and out of the house as he pleased. As our co-existence grew, I realized I was ready for a real pet. A loving soul… so, what else, a dog! I wanted my own baby again.

Given our living space, and the cat, I decided I wanted a small dog. I hemmed and hawed, but as I talked more about it, I learned of a woman named Cinnamon who worked in the same company as me and fostered rescues. Get this – she only worked with small dogs. In September 2005, I made an appointment to see the new crop of rescues that came in. I always knew animals pick their humans. Be it cat or dog, whenever I have gone to a shelter or even a shop – the animal that is meant to be mine, the one I bond with, has always reached for me. Endlessly. It is how they picked me. Cinnamon was so moved by this story that she gave me first pick.

Lessons Learned from My Rescue Dog

So, on September 1st, when I went to Cinnamon's house to see if any of the puppies would pick me, I saw Natalie. Now, Natalie was undeniably beautiful. And yet she bore a remarkable resemblance to Ashley. So remarkable that my heart skipped a beat and I couldn't catch my breath. I asked about her, and Cinnamon told me she had some liver issues and they were not sure if they would go away or if I would need to nurse her for the rest of her life. Add to that that she was already five years old, was undernourished, and was vomiting every day. Huh. So, I guess the resemblance was more than just looks. I did not pick her up. I had already been down that road and I just couldn't bring myself to get back into that situation again. So, I picked up a few of the others – and I honestly would have taken any and all of them home.

And then Natalie was near me… and this little voice in my head said, "Just pick her up and look into her eyes. You can always put her down." So I did. And when I went to pick up the next puppy, she started to climb my leg. I looked at Cinnamon… and she looked at me. We both knew: "Well, I guess I have been picked." It was that simple. Natalie picked me. And in that moment, I knew no matter what, I would bring her home, I would take care of her, and she would be my baby.

What I didn't know was how bonded we got in that one instant when we looked into each other's eyes. I brought her home, and within two days, my now ex-husband and I were to go out of town for our anniversary weekend. We did not want the weekend to be about her, so we left her with my in-laws. I thought of Natalie every hour. I just wanted to be with her. And apparently, she just wanted to be with me. When we returned, my then-mother in law said that she would not eat without me. And with every passing car, she ran to see if it were me. When we reunited, she did her happy dance. She would get into the downward dog yoga position, which by the way could not have been better named. With her butt high, tail wagging, and a goofy grin, she would tap her feet then turn clockwise. Two taps and a turn. Again and again until I talked to her, tapped the floor with her and picked her up. It was the cutest little dance. And she waited for me to participate in this dance. It was her happy dance. It was the first time I saw this… and again, it was remarkably similar to Ashley.

Now, you may think I am saying that this was Ashley reincarnated. My answer is an emphatic No. Ashley was Ashley. Natalie is and will always be my princess. My Natalie. I was able to nurse her back to health. We got her teeth cleaned up, which ultimately meant the removal of many of them. This meant that her food had to be soft, and of course, I indulged. With that and the help of some supplements, her liver enzyme counts went down. And for a good long time, she was my healthy, happy, dance-y, demanding little princess. For a long time, I truly believed she picked me because she knew I would take care of her; that I was her momma. What I did not realize at the time was that she was actually my sweet angel. She knew she had to take care of me. And that is why she picked me. Not for what I could do for her, but what she was destined to do for me.

Relationships between a pet and their human are deep and so very personal. But when you rescue an animal, that ends up being a deeper connection for the human as well as the animal. The animal is so grateful and becomes part of your soul; and you theirs.

How can twelve years seem so long and so short all at once? Natty and I were together for only twelve years. In the larger scheme of my life, that is not too long. So far is it a little more than a fifth of my life. But for Natty, that was two-thirds of her life. And while I may want to hold myself in the highest esteem for rescuing her, the reality is she rescued me. She enriched my life. And she continues to permeate every aspect of my life that I hold most dear. How can one little creature that weighed six pounds do so much? I need to stop kidding myself. Rescuing her was just not that. She rescued me. She watched over me.

Natty and Food

Food is not merely sustenance for everyone. For many people, it is an emotional supplement. Often food offers us comfort, security, and even happiness. Personally, I have struggled with this. I have eaten out of frustration, happiness, sadness, and despair. And when those emotions subside, the food doesn't always follow the pattern. My food habits, both good and bad, are formed easily and stay long after the emotion is gone. In fact, I have eaten so very many emotions that I cannot recall the first emotion I ate. I have since learned that if hunger is not my problem, then eating food is not my solution. But what was most interesting to me was that dogs overeat too – and not just because they are silly dogs that do not know their limits. They are not just gluttonous creatures. No, they eat their anxiety and insecurities as well. Of course, I learned this with Natty.

The only back-story I got on her was that she was living on the street with a couple of other dogs and a homeless person. This person used her as bait when begging for money. Naturally, Natalie was fairly undernourished and had terrible teeth when I got her. In fact, she was in such ill health that I wasn't sure how ong I would have her. As it turned out, she had terrible liver enzyme issues and she vomited at least twice a day at first. Getting her to eat was always a challenge. I started out with getting her teeth cleaned up. That process left her with so few chewing teeth that I had to prepare soft foods for her. So I started cooking her special meals. Luckily, Cinnamon, the sweet lady that fostered Natalie was super helpful in this department. In fact, she even sent us home with a meal.

Bowzer, our curmudgeonly cat, was unaffected by her presence. That is of course, until she tried to eat some of his wet food. At which point Bowzer (who was by the way eighteen pounds to Natty's then five pounds) gave Natty three - yes, three! - swift slaps on the face. I jumped to save my new baby. She had the most beautiful huge eyes that just popped out at you. He could have scratched one! But good old Natalie just took it in stride. She understood. Bowzer's food was his, and I would jump to protect her at all costs. And the bonus lesson for me – she likes cat food.

So, I cooked for my puppy child. And she ate it. But, never the same meal two times in a row, and when she was done with this homemade concoction, she was done. With some supplements, clean teeth, and her special diet, she got better. She stopped vomiting and she gained weight! What a relief. The doctor told us that 6-7 pounds was her ideal weight. So when she hit that, we celebrated and weaned her off her special diet. We tried everything else. We tried the kidney food, we tried doctoring the kidney food, we tried some cooked food, some kidney food... any combo we tried, she hated. She literally would be starving and would refuse to eat. This little girl ate what she wanted to eat. Finally we found some grocery store brand of wet food that she liked, so we stocked up. And she gained weight. She went up to 9 pounds! Now, 2 pounds more on you or me is just a bad day. But 2 pounds on a pup of her size is massive. It seemed to me she ate her insecurities in food. And then my ex and I separated. And when she realized he was not coming back, it was like she instantly let go of her anxiety and never went above 6.3 pounds again.

Seeing Natty process her anxiety gave me the realization that food is not a substitute for our insecurities. If we waiver and it is for a short time, when that time comes to an end, so should our related food habits.

It took a few years, but I eventually weaned her off of the liver supplements. And her checkups went from quarterly to semi-annually, and finally to annually. I faithfully had her teeth cleaned and made sure she had every checkup, every shot, everything she needed to stay healthy. Along with that, she also got to eat any food she desired. So, if I went out for steak, which I ended to do a couple times a month, I would always order enough for my Natty bag. And she would feast on filet mignon and baked potato for two days. If she felt like she was over-eating, she would not eat for one meal, and then return to her normal eating. She was self-regulating.

I did not always understand her behavior. But she knew what she wanted, and she knew when she wanted it. And most importantly, she knew when to stop. I fussed and fumbled and took the longest time to figure out that she instinctively knew. She knew when eating was the answer. She knew when a nap or a cuddle was better than food. And she always knew eating with people around was better than eating alone.

Don't get me wrong, she still went crazy for a fast food burger and she absolutely loved bread. But I think that came from years of being on the street. I think that is the food she was given. But more than anything, my little Natalie loved to savor her food with her pack. And being with her pack was important to her. I used to say she loved eating for an audience. But really, she would eat only when she was with her pack or her people. Left to her own devices, she was less interested. When I later rescued another dog named Dolly, Natty would eagerly start eating her food, but always made sure that

Lessons Learned from My Rescue Dog

Dolly was taken care of and would pause to see that sh
got her food.

Just like all of us, she thought food tasted better witl
company. You get to socialize and savor your food. An
if you are with your loved ones, then food becomes
happy celebration. It stops being about our insecuritie
and our lacking. It becomes what it is – sustenance -
for life. And for love.

Why We Have Pets

When Natty passed, I had a lot of well wishers telling me that she would always be around me, and that maybe some day in the future she may even show up as another pet in my life. This spurred a bunch of thoughts on Natty and why she entered my life and how she may show up again.

The thing is, I believe in reincarnation. I was brought up believing this, and even when I questioned my own religion, I never questioned reincarnation. I have come to believe that we are like a tree… we are the base and the bigger branches are our core people - those that are closest to us. Some of those smaller branches are the people in our outer circles, but they are still part of our lives. And just like with humans, I believe that this was not her first life. Taking that to the next step, I am likely not her only tree - and for that matter, I am not her only tree branch. And even if I was, I believe that her life is sacred and most importantly hers. I believe she is meant to have more tree limbs and leaves and really so many more connections. I also hope that she is taking the time to rest for now and when she is ready, she will re-enter the world and touch other people's lives as she touched mine. That said, I do believe that our souls will cross paths again. I just do not believe she is my only dog, nor that I am her only human. Who knows, maybe in our next crossing, we will exchange roles.

Now that makes me stop and think… I sure am glad I loved her so dearly and indulged her so completely!

But back to why we have pets… There is that saying that someone comes into your life for a reason, a season, or a lifetime. Natty came into my life when she was already five years old. And she stayed with me for twelve short, great years. But, she will be with me for the rest of my life. At the very least, she certainly influenced my lifetime. She will never be forgotten. After all, it is because of her that I am so happy and safe. And because of her that we got Dolly. And because of her that Glenn is in my life. And because of her that Dolly loves Emma, a cat we later adopted, so very much.

While Glenn is an amazing person, and I really feel like I am living in a fairy tale, there was a time or two when I wondered if it would last. And had it not been for Natty, it may not have. They loved each other so much, sometimes I wondered if he didn't stay with me because of her. They were instantly connected, as if each were the other's tree limb that had been missing for so long. There is no way I could have broken her heart and ever let him go. She loved him so completely.

Trusted him so sweetly. No matter how much she had been hurt before, when she loved, she loved fully.

Usually, it took her time to get to know someone. The first time most people walked into the house, she would bark. That is, unless I was holding her and let her know that the person coming in was a friend. And even then, it took her time to watch and trust the people. But once she trusted, she loved. Completely.

However, even if she trusted you she was still a picky eater. Very few people in her life could get her to eat. Even I struggled with it. And yet she ate for Glenn more than anyone else. Even me. When we went out of town, whoever took care of her would always say that she would not eat. Even if one of us was out of town, the other struggled with getting her to eat. Food wasn't her comfort. We were. Her purpose, if she had one, was to love us and to be with us both. In the end, all she wanted was for us to all be in one room so she could see her whole family. She would usher me, Glenn, Dolly and even Emma into the room. Her favorite time was when we were all on the bed with her. Only then would she close her eyes and rest. If she had a purpose, it was only to love and be with her family.

As I think about the best times in my life, I realize that they are not the big celebrations, they are in these little everyday moments. It is in the way we are with

Why We Have Pets

our friends and family. The best times in our lives are in how we spend time with our people. It is in how we love them. And that is our purpose... to be with and love our people.

Keep Calm, and Walk
at Your Own Pace

Have you ever done a 5k? 10k? Half marathon? Full marathon? Ever done any race? What I mean to ask is – have you ever run against the clock? Did you ever realize that in running, as in any endeavor, it takes an intense desire to improve? Especially when people are passing you by and really all you can do is move at your pace. If you sprint now, you may run out of steam. And what if you don't want to sprint? What if you want to amble along? Is it ok to not even look like you want to move faster? Is it ok to just calmly mosey? I suppose it is just fine to amble if there is no clock. And even if there is. Even if there are people passing you by, and others rushing you to move faster, when you ignore it all, that is what I like to call blocking out the noise.

Ms. Natty, she moved at her own pace. Even in her prime. She ran when she wanted and walked when she wanted. There were even times that she was quite cat-like and would not even get up when called. And she could really run – when she felt like it. She moved when she wanted; and for her own reasons. There was one time, we had just brought Dolly home. Dolly understood, you go out to the backyard, do your

19

business and come running back inside – especially in the rain. Natty however, she moved at her own pace. Always. Even at my urging, Natty just ambled along. So, Dolly took it upon herself to 'round her up.' To that end, Dolly would run circles around Natty. Literally. Big circles. Her circles were the width of the entire backyard. As Natty walked the length of the lawn from back to front, Dolly would run around her in hopes of getting her to move faster. If she'd been less afraid of Natty, I think she would have actually literally nudged her along from behind. But she just ran circles around her… making her circles shorter and more towards the house… edging it up from behind. This was all to encourage Natty to move forward, to move faster, to get out of the rain. The thing is, Natty just wanted to march to her own beat. My urgency, rain, cold, nothing mattered to Natty as much as her own beat; listening to herself and knowing what her pace ought to be.

Don't get me wrong, the girl could run! She was known to take off at a full gallop when the mood struck. In fact, we once did a Furry 5k. A friend and I decided to do this with our dogs. We were helping raise money for a local animal shelter. Dolly was of course afraid of so many animals, but she faithfully followed Ms. Natty. There we were, two adults, and 4 dogs. Natty was the smallest and was on a mission. She led the pack, or at least her pack. She went the entire 5k without stopping. Other dogs were bigger and ran past her. She couldn't have cared less. She just kept her nose down and went at her own pace. Of course, since she was our leader, we went at her pace too.

Sometimes just moving forward takes everything you have in your whole body. And sometimes you just need to take your time and savor where you are. It really doesn't matter what kind of urging you get from anyone. The noise of people passing you by doesn't matter nearly as much as what feels right to you. You just need to close your mind to comparing yourself to others.

And I find that this lesson is good for just about everything. Any journey we take – be it an actual race, finding the love of our life, weight loss -- you name it, this lesson applies. Hold your own. Ignore the noise. Keep moving forward. Go at your own pace.

It is OK to Have a Favorite... a Connection

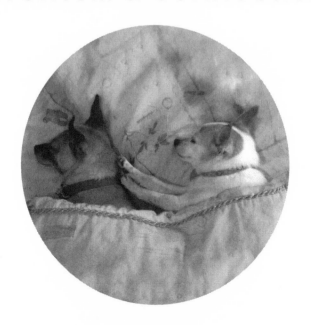

I hear parents say this all the time – I love my kids equally. Or they have to be fair to both their kids. I one kid gets music lessons, then the other one should too. And yet, I wonder, is it really what both kids want. What if one kid wants to sing and one wants to dance? Or what if one wants play an instrument and one wants to ride his or her bike? And even if they both did different activities, what if one just wanted to stay home and play video games, but the other wanted to play instruments and dance? Where is the balance between knowing what your kid wants and imposing what you want for your kid onto their lives? But I digress… really, I am thinking about the connections we have with children. Whether they are our own children or whether they are adopted or not ours at all. And sometimes, our pets are our children. Sometimes they pick us, and sometimes we pick them.

In the case of Natty, she picked me. And it was as if by some strange magic, I knew what she was thinking. I knew when she was mad at me. I immediately knew the difference in her bark – whether it was coming from fear, or primal protection. To this day, I do not feel like I was imposing my thoughts or beliefs onto her. I never felt nor do I feel like I was projecting my thoughts or emotions on her. Make no mistake about it, she was my mirror; she was my mini-me, my shadow, my echo. We just had a connection. A very special connection... we were intertwined. If I was sick, she was glued to my side. If she was sick... I was the worst helicopter mom that any vet saw.

And when we got Dolly, I got her so that Natty would have a purpose. Goodness knows she had already trained me, so she needed her new challenge. And to be perfectly honest, I was a little worried she was getting up there in age. If I got a new puppy, logic states that she would help train the dog, and the dog would maybe even take on some quintessential Natty characteristics.

So we went to pick out a new puppy. It took us three puppies at three different locations to find the first one that honored her status while pushing Natty to love and accept her. And even then, I swear for two months all Natty "said" – in that big cartoon air bubble above her head – was, "Really momma, why did we need a *dog*? Of all things... a dog?!? We were perfectly happy just the two of us. And if we really had to, we could have at least gotten a cat." But true to the pack dogma, Natty trained Dolly. And Dolly became a great dog. A truly great dog. And to this day, Dolly is a dog. She never took to being a princess. Don't get me wrong, she loves her attention. She loves her dresses – it gives her a great sense of belonging. Not to mention, she loves the attention her dresses bring her on our walks. So basically, to keep to our majestic theme, Dolly was our beloved duchess.

But that connection I had with Natty... that innate "I know her, I recognize her" is just not there with my Doll. Do not misunderstand, I adore my sweet duchess dog. But it begs the question... where is the innate connection with this soul?

A couple of years ago, we decided we wanted another puppy. But after much discussion, we decided it would be a cat. Introducing a cat would help to calm Dolly. After all, as the dog of the house, she went nuts when she saw one. We figured Natty would teach her to be nice to the cat and it would be fun. So, we found Emma.

The very second I saw her, I picked her. Nothing like the story with Natty mind you, but when I saw her, I knew she was my baby. She was in someone else's arms, and I just had to hold her. It took all of my strength not to snatch her away. I maintained my composure and asked the young girl if I could hold her. I then covertly asked the lady working there if the other girl was truly going to adopt her. She put my worries to rest – no. Whew. I knew. I *knew* that this was my baby kitten. She was friendly, beautiful and sweet. I knew Natty would love her!

It is OK to Have a Favorite... a Connection

Oh sure, there were other friendly, sweet, beautiful kittens around. All equal in those traits. But Emma... there was just an immediate connection. I just knew Emma was my baby. So, we got her. Turns out she ended up being both my baby and Glenn's. Which is absolutely perfect, because I adopted Natty and Dolly before I met him, and the reason we went looking for a third baby was that we wanted to adopt one together. And so this connection that we have with Emma grows. We absolutely love our Doll. There is nothing we wouldn't do for her, but somehow that bond is there with Emma. That innate connection with both of us. We won't ever say that we love one more than the other. But whip out our phones, look in our photo albums, and you will see. The day we brought Em home, she dominated our photos. Even above Natty. The connection was so strong.

I come back to wondering, is this a situation of soul recognition? Did we just know her from before? Is this connection any different than say an aunt who has a favorite niece or nephew? Why was I closer to my aunt and uncle than my brother was? Was it just that I had more contact? Was it all circular? Or was there something else there? Could it be that we have more than one soul mate? That our nearest and dearest come back and join us in our journey time and again?

Lessons Learned from My Rescue Dog

I always thought of my life as a tree. The large branches are the souls that are closest to me... the smaller branches are new souls. Could Natty be one of my big branches? As I get older, I wonder... are those larger branches really taken up by nuclear family members? Or are they just the souls we love the most in this world?

After feeling the connections with my animals, would say that there is something; a bond formed in that first moment, where you just know. You recognize that you know this soul. You have always known this soul. And you will forever know this soul. And when the puppies you adopt along the way show up next time, you will recognize them again. Because you are their favorite. And that is better than ok. It is wonderful.

Natty at the Beach, Park, and Hiking

Natty loved smelling things. In truth, I would say mostly she loved smelling outside, but that is likely because she was used to the scents inside. Except when we came home. She was particularly good at instinctively knowing when we had eaten while we were out. We would have to lightly blow towards her face so she could smell our breath. It was much like you blow in a horse's nose to let them get to know you. And then, once she sussed out her version of the details, she would either be fine (if we ate sushi) or would go nuts wanting to know where her portion was (especially if we had steak).

Taking Nat on a walk – especially to the dog park – was one of the most interesting experiences I had with her. I would take her to the little dog section where she could safely be off leash. The first time I did this, I hovered around her because she was truly smaller than 95% of the "small" dogs in there. But Natty did not care whether I or in fact any other dog or person was there. She made a beeline to the farthest side of the park and started sniffing the perimeter. When she was done, I was hoping she would socialize a little, but instead, she decided that she had to make another smaller round.

And she maintained this laser focus, circling the area again and again until her circles got small enough to hit center. When she was done smelling everything, she was done. Not one dog could make her lose focus. When one tried, she scoffed at him and went on with her sniffing routine. I swear that dog just walked away baffled. So when Natty finished her sniff-fest, she ran back to me and was ready to go home. That was all she needed from her experience. She did not care to socialize with other dogs, because really she was not one herself. And she already knew all the business without having to sniff the doggies' butts!

On the other hand, taking Natty hiking was like watching a bird play in the air. She absolutely loved wide-open spaces. She would run randomly from here to there and just keep going. Watching her in an open field was the best – she was like a field rat that had no purpose other than to enjoy the space she had. And she reveled in it. And yet, when we went on a hike, she would lead us. She would be about 10 steps ahead and would make sure I was within earshot. She always loved just smelling the path. If we came back the same way, she would simply smell the other side of the path with equal diligence. Taking the same hike 2 days in a row would not change this behavior. There were too many new smells to check out. It was almost as of the smells were not just bread crumbs telling her where she was and how to get back, but also served as some kind of news story. Like another animal's scent was not just their scent, but also the latest gossip. What was happening and what was going to happen. And Natty marking on that spot was not a simple act of relief or even dominance, but as an update to her news story. So, when we would go the next day, she naturally had to check on all the updates.

One day, we went to the beach. Granted, we lived in the Pacific Northwest, so for us, it meant going a rather cold part of the coastline in Oregon. The first time we took her to beach, I knew she would love it. There were so many different smells that are so vastly different than that of the woods. And how right I was. That girl loved the breeze, the sand in her paws, and running free and wild. Luckily, I could see how far she was going and there was nowhere for her to hide. She had the ocean on one side, and the sandbank on the other. I knew she did not like going into water from when we took her to the lake. She liked to be by the water, she even tolerated being on the water. But God forbid her lovely fur get wet… she would not have it. Unless of course it was to get a bath, because she loved her fur being clean. But I digress… so, while I was prepared for her to not go anywhere near the ocean water, I had no idea how far she would take it.

There was a tiny stream from a recent rain that ran the length of the beach. It went all the way from the sand bank to the ocean. Towards the ocean, it was smaller, but as you got to the sandbank, it actually became about 2 feet wide. As a rational human, I simply walked over it. And truthfully, had Natty been a rational dog, she would have done the same. But she was so insistent that she would not get wet, that she decided to run the entire length of the beach and back before she barked to let us know she would absolutely not cross this "river," for she will not walk on water, through or over it. And goodness knows, if we wanted her to come with us, we would need to give her a lift over this "stream" of water. And so I walked over to her. As if to punctuate her dire straits, when I picked her up, she spread each of her paws to their farthest reach. As if to underscore the importance that none of her paws should get even a drop of the water. She literally did a full spread eagle with every limb. It was… well, it was hysterical. No matter how hard I laughed, or even the extra time it took for me to pose for a photo, she stayed spread out like that. She wanted to be absolutely certain that no unintended water touched her gorgeous fur.

Now, I know what you are thinking… She was a prissy little girl that I catered to far too much. It wasn't really like that. We would call her our little field rat because she absolutely loved to wander around all over. She even liked to hike. All said, she was a darling soul that knew what she liked and what she wanted. And she was fierce. She would step in front of any animal

or person and find her big scary bark just to protec
someone she loved.

And if you saw the love in her eyes… you would do
it too. Because there was nothing sweeter than thi
little puppy looking up and me with gratitude, love
understanding, and happiness. To know her was to
truly love her. To love her was to indulge her. And to
be loved by her was to feel like you were cherished
protected and always loved.

Natty Catches a Fly – in her mouth! Karate Kid Style!

Be patient; act once. Definitively. Measure twice, cut once. All of these are great pieces of advice. In one quick ninja move, Natalie demonstrated this lesson.

We were on a road trip from Montana to Seattle. It had been a long trip, much of it spent in the car. We had just spent the afternoon with a family member that had Alzheimer's, so we were reflective and mostly quiet, looking forward to getting home. We were racing down the I-90 headed west towards home. Personally, I love road trips. And as long as we were on the freeway and the windows were rolled up, so did Natty. The thing is, we had the windows down when we were saying goodbye to the family. We rolled them up as soon as we got on the freeway. However, we inadvertently trapped a fly in the car with us. So, we rolled one window down, then the next, then both. One attempt after another to remove that fly failed. To note, we were still speeding along at a modest clip of 80mph. So, when one window went down, it produced a sound akin to banging on one ear. And when both were down, the wind beat both ears. At some point, we realized that it was less painful to live with the fly buzzing around our ears, so we just rolled the windows up. But it was one of those really loud, annoying flies. So we started our process again. Still no luck. Eventually we pulled over. Opened the door, looked for the fly. It simply disappeared. We thought it flew away. But it was a sly one. Or maybe it was just playing with us? We started down the freeway again. Bzzzz…. Bzzzzz…. bzzzz. Oh crap – it was still in the car. Even with music, it had no problem making itself heard. It was like the little bugger would find our ears and intentionally buzz into them. So, we started the window routine again.

If this story seems long, believe me when I tell you it was a solid hour before we finally gave up. And the next time we heard it buzz, Natty looked at me, looked at the fly, lifted her head, opened her mouth, snapped at the fly – which promptly fell dead beside her little body – and put her head back down. She gave me one look as if to say, "And that's how it's done," before letting her eyelids drop and dozing off.

I was dumbfounded. In a second, she gave me her best withering stare, as if to say, "If I take care of it, can we just keep driving home without all the drama?" Then she snapped and killed the little bugger. I have certainly seen frogs do this, but 1. They ate the fly; and 2. Natty was a dog. I will never know if she was more annoyed by the fly or by our antics. Either way, she was thoughtful, calculated and precise in her actions. She did not fuss about for an hour and fail. She observed, she became present in the moment, and she acted decisively.

I wonder what in my life I have hemmed and hawed about. What have I floundered about that couldn't have been solved with some calm observation and a swift kick of action? How much time and energy have I wasted? How much have I spun around an issue? What could I have done with that time? Thanks to the lesson I learned from Natty, I've become more present and definitely more decisive in taking action. Thanks, Natty!

Lesson learned: The more you freak out about something, the harder it is to get done.

Natty Was My Child and Always Will Be

There was an unmistakable bond between Natty and me. There was no denying it. From the moment I held her in my hands she knew. It was startling because she was so shy that Cinnamon, her foster mom, did not think she would let me so much as hold her. I put her down briefly to pick up her brother, but she started to climb up my leg, and I knew. We all knew. Especially Natty.

I brought her home to my then-husband and his cat. We had decided to adopt to commemorate our anniversary. I was never supposed to fall in love with a dog so quickly. Especially since within a couple of days, we were scheduled to go out of town. I was not away from Natty for more than 20 hours, but my then-in-laws said she looked for me with every passing car. She wouldn't eat, barely drank any water, and just looked out the window for me. I know they were trying to tell me she loved me so much already. But really, it just broke my heart. I felt guilty that I left her. So, after that, I got in the habit of taking her with me on my trips or telling her where I was going and when I would be back. I know it sounds weird, but she really seemed to understand. And so our pattern was set. I talked to her and treated her as if she were my child.

Natty Was My Child and Always Will Be

As a woman of a certain age, people always asked when I was going to have a child. And now that I was married, they felt more compelled to ask even louder. So, when I adopted Natty and announced her to friends and family as the child I adopted, they got very excited for me. And then very disappointed when my adopted child turned out to be a dog. Of course, knowing the prankster that I am, most people just let it go. And kept letting it go. Though some actually refused to accept that there was a bond. Most people just disregarded that there was a real relationship, although my friends who met Natty and saw us together could see our bond.

And as I think about most of my friends who are parents to fur babies, I know their bond is no different than mine to Natty. Our fur babies are our cherished children. We love them, worry for them, take care of them, clean them, so on and so forth. However, we are often disregarded simply because our children have 4 legs and fur. The thing is, we will almost certainly outlive our fur babies. So, taking on a pet is pure act of love. We know we will likely lose them before we are ready. But the truth about having children is that sometimes the choice is made for us, and sometimes we make the choice ourselves.

There was a time in my life when I wanted to have children. I even had names picked out. For me, it was a foregone conclusion that I would have children. And then I found out I could not have children. At the time it did not bother me – by this point, I was no longer married. And that desire just left me. I did not want to have children any longer. I assumed it would return when I was no longer alone. But as time went on, I wondered if the desire would ever return. And then I realized, I really only wanted the feeling of a family; I wanted a partner, and I wanted to mentor children. But the actual thought of having my own children just never came back.

Andy Dooley says, "Feeling first, manifestation second." Since relationships were eluding me at the time I decided to go after the feeling I wanted… the family feeling. I was looking into mentoring, and my friend told me about a dog foster that had a bunch of dogs coming in. I felt ready to look into it. Plus, the synchronicity of it was perfect. So, I went… and I found Natty. Or more accurately, she found me.

And we had the bond instantly. That familial bond. That bond that was so real, that any time it was discounted felt like complete disregard and judgment to me. Sadly, many times, it felt like this. All because she was not human. Though claiming my fur babies as my children garnered even more judgment. But how could I explain that this was about my _feelings_? I felt connected to Natty. And she felt connected to me and others in my life. In the end, why couldn't we be accepted as a amily? This is not something you need to explain to hose who have chosen fur babies as their only babies. n fact, we are not displacing our emotions. It is love. It s pure love. The feelings are there. Why judge it?

As I write this story and think back on it, I realize hat maybe I was judging those that judged me. I wonder if I'd cared less, if what they thought would have bothered me less. But those who really judged me did not know Natty. And for that matter did not know me. For those who know me... my friends... my ribe... those people, needed no explanation. Whether hey had human children or not, all beings are love. And we understand that all love is beyond judgement. All feelings of love are good. For all creatures. Because he point to life is to live it... in love.

Natty and the Doggy Door

When we lived in Seattle, we lived in a lovely and safe neighborhood. So safe, we would leave the back door open as we slept in the summers. It just never got hot enough to install central air conditioning. So we would all enjoy the cooler night air. At some point, we decided to put in a little swinging kitty door into the screen so that Natty and Dolly could go in and out as they pleased. They were both small enough to get in and out a kitty door which made self-installation worth it. It saved us from having to get up in the middle of the night to open the door. Even so, it was a cumbersome install and took some doing. But in the end, we got it done. Unfortunately, we got it installed on what ended up being a chilly rainy evening. And yet, we still figured we could teach Ms. Natty how to use it. Sadly, she had other ideas. We tried to swing the door through and show her that she could walk through it. But she simply did not want to go. Pushing her through it just seemed cruel. No matter how we tried, she just would not push through. In retrospect, I wonder if the struggle of installation had an effect on her. Or maybe, she just did not want to use it because it was made for animals and she truly believed she was human.

Eventually, we decided to give her a break and try to teach Dolly how to use the door... so, we tried, and she went through. We were so thrilled for her. And quite honestly, a little perplexed. Dolly is an adorable puppy... sweet and loyal as the day is long, but not nearly as smart as Natty. Also, she took all her cues from Natty. So, how did she forge through before Natty?? We called her to get her to come back in so she could see it worked both ways. She was all smiles and tail waggy-ness. But then she saw Natty's withering stare and realized that she did something wrong. That was that. Dolly would not come in for anything. We tried treats, we tried calling her, we tried swinging the door open. She just stared at the imposing barrier that was Natty. Eventually, we had to open the screen door to let her back in.

It was getting late, and we had plans to go out for a nice steak dinner with friends that evening. So, we put the lessons aside, brought Dolly in the old way, and went out for dinner. We hoped that giving Natty a few hours would reset her stubbornness. Thankfully, it was indeed a steak dinner we went out to, so we figured leftovers would help entice our little princess into going in and out of the swing door. We set out to try with Natty again. We put some steak in a little dish just outside the swing door. We tried to entice her, but she just would not go... so, then we reversed it. And all she did was tuck her tail, and stand out there in the rain. And stand there she did for a few minutes... then she went down the stairs and hung out under the deck so she didn't get quite so wet. When we found her, we were not sure whether to laugh at her or feel guilty as all get out for "throwing her out." She looked like a wet rat dog - pathetic and dripping wet. So, we meticulously dried her off and called it a night.

The next day, the rain dried out and we had the door open again. Suddenly, Natty decided she had to pee... and I ran to open the screen door for her, only to find her tapping the swing screen with her paw a few times. I stopped short and held my breath. I was hopeful she would push through and go out that way. As it swung inwards, she used her nose to push it up and walk through and have it swing shut behind her. She basically opened the door and went through it, much like every human does. We open our doors, walk through, then close it. Wait, what?!?! She was throwing a full fit because she did not want to use her nose to push forward through it? Apparently, she wanted the door to be opened for her and was willing to figure out how to open it for herself. After that, she always pawed the door and went through it like a civilized lady dog....

Of course, like the sweet beta dog that she is, once Dolly saw that Natty was using the door, she too started to use it again. But Dolly did it nose first. Like a dog.

Natty and the Doggy Door

Natty's obstinacy could be seen even in her walks. Ordinarily, she was a good walker. She loved to walk the neighborhood, smell the smells and mark her path. But every once in a while, she needed to dig her nose deep into that one bush that she just had to smell. Her claws would dig into the unforgiving cement and all 6 pounds of her would lean into her pull. At times like those, there was no moving beyond that spot until she was good and ready to move. It just had to be her way.

In truth, we should have known…. Natty is not, nor was ever a "dog"… we always knew she was a princess. She was headstrong and at the very same time, dainty and lady-like. She just needed to do it her way. She never went nose first through the kitty door, and never passed up a bush she wanted to smell.

I think about that choice to live your life so deliberately. Owning my life experiences so much that I do what I want when I want. Knowing that even the chores of my life are choices that I make. There is an incredible freedom in living life in this manner. And there is strength in it too. To always stand up and say, "This is what I want. This is my life," can sometimes mean life is about tradeoffs. As much as Natty loved steak, that night she wouldn't eat it because she didn't want to go nose first through the kitty door. And yet, aren't those tradeoffs worth it? To own your own life so completely. To live for yourself can only make you stronger to be there for your loved ones. To love more completely. Because when you understand self-love... you understand all love.

Natty the Guard Dog

As soon as she entered the house, Ms. Natty decided she was the guard dog. Yes… the tiny underweight dog thought she was in charge of me and everyone else in the house, plus the house. So sure, she barked up a storm if anyone came to the house – especially if they came in the house and she didn't know them. Though, to be fair, she was also the welcoming committee. If someone she knew entered the house, she would do her happy dance and would not stop until shown some love.

But, back to her guarding duties… She would keep guard looking out the big picture window. And if anyone dared to cross in front of the house when we were not home, she would bark her little heart out… For that matter, if we were home, she would bark even louder. She just wanted to protect her people from all outside elements. Eventually, I figured it out… if I was home and someone was coming into the house, I had to scoop the little thing up in my arms so she could smell the person before they crossed into her domain. She was so tiny, most people just figured I was that crazy dog lady that indulged her tiny pup. Everyone expected her to be a "barky" dog because she was such a tiny Chihuahua. Don't get me wrong, she barked, but she was not unnecessarily yippy. There was intention behind her bark. And there was heft... her bark belied her size. It was that of a larger dog... well, not a large dog, but when you heard her bark, you would not have thought it came from a tiny thing. She, as some would say, found her voice. Or in this case, her bark.

We kept our back door open in the summers and one fine day, Dolly decided to go out in the middle of the night. We heard her cry from the back yard and I got up with a start. That was not a normal Dolly noise. Glenn groggily told me that I was overreacting and then in what seemed like slow motion, he realized that truly this noise was not a good Dolly sound. So up he jumped, large flashlight in hand, running out the back shouting that I should close the screen door behind him. So I closed the screen door thinking that would be good enough. But of course, there was the doggy door. And Ms. Natty decided to run out. So now, Glenn was standing at the top of the deck with a huge search light going back and forth across the backyard and little Ms. six-pound Natty was right by his side. Seeing her daddy in distress, she started to bark. Mind you, her bark wasn't idly saying, "Come in Glenn, let's go back to sleep," or "Dork-a-Dolly, come towards my bark... it's still sleepy time," or even, "Dumb Dolly, it is not play in the yard time, it is sleepy time." Rather, her bark was fierce. It did not even sound like her. It sounded like she was saying, "Whatever is out there, I warn you, I am here and I will protect that stupid idiot dog that is in my yard."

So to review, fifteen-pound Dolly is outside, distressed; Glenn is shining a spot light on her and yelling at me to get Natty inside. I am yelling at Natty to come with me, while she keeps running back and forth and is evading my grasp, and Natty is still barking fiercely. Then out of the darkness, Dolly darted into the line of light, followed closely by one very large raccoon. Now I mean very large; easily twice the size of Dolly with opposable thumbs! Suddenly, all I could see was these black gloved hands reaching for; nearly grasping for Dolly's tail as Dolly is taking the stairs up towards us two at a time. Thanks to the huge flashlight and Glenn's swift thinking, he shone the light in the raccoon's eyes and apparently blinded it for a second. The raccoon lost its footing and fell off the stairs. He scampered off and just like that the noise ended… we all filed into the house silently.

The next morning, we were all emotionally and physically spent. We did nothing. We just sat in one space or another… bed to couch and back to bed again… touching each other. So glad for the roles each of us played… so glad for everyone. That raccoon had no idea that this family of four would stand up to him… and that we would stand up for each other. And the fact that we were led by this little six pound fury-filled puppy made no difference. The fact is, it didn't matter that Natty was the tiniest character in this scenario. To be clear, she was half the size of Dolly, one sixth the size of the raccoon, a fraction the size of her humans. But in her soul, she knew she was big enough. She knew her bark was enough to help. She knew only she could protect us. She knew she was part of the team. She believed so strongly that she was the heart, soul and protector that she had to be in the middle of it. So, any unwelcome guests were hereforth warned… be it in front of the window, or in our backyard… no one messes with one of Natty's family members.

That is what Natty taught me… it is not the size of the person. It is the size of the love in your heart. More than that, it is the belief in yourself.

No Paparazzi!

have talked a lot about the great big personality Ms. Natty had. But don't get me wrong, she was a gorgeous animal. She had incredibly soft fur; big brown eyes, and stunning dark brown eyelids. Once, someone actually asked me if I had tattooed her to make it look like she was wearing eyeliner! She was that kind of beautiful. Oh, and she had the most adorable sable marking right above her left leg –when she curled up in her napping ball, it looked like a heart. Yes, my little Natty had what I affectionately referred to as a heart tramp stamp. No, no, her heart was just so big, she wore it on the outside.

Given how absolutely gorgeous she was, it still came as a huge surprise to me that she was such a brilliant actress. When I first adopted her, she was fairly ill and her teeth were so bad, she needed extensive cleanings and extractions. But first, she needed to get some vaccinations. I was to take her home and watch her carefully to make sure she was ok. I was told she could be a little lethargic, but nothing to truly concern myself with. And so, when I brought her home, and she wasn't bouncy, I was ok. But when she wouldn't eat, I started to worry. Then I quickly recalled the vet tech saying that she may have a reduced appetite. So, I left her food there for her to eat and made my own dinner. She walked over to me and was limping. At first I thought I was seeing things. Then, she started to limp even more… and then she started carrying her hind leg up completely hopping; using only 3 legs.

I absolutely freaked out. Complete. Freak. Out. I had completely bonded with this soul, and now she was broken. I put my plate down, and I called the vet and talking a mile a minute, I told them what was going on. They tried to calm me and explain that there was probably some pain at the injection site, but she was going to be fine. I was still fairly inconsolable, but then I spied Natty balancing strongly on her hind legs. On her hind legs. She was reaching for my dinner. Huh… I guess she was fine, just acting because she thought I would give her some of my steak rather than her chicken. Wait, what?!? She was acting? And here I was nearly screaming at the vet? With a heavy sigh, and my tail tucked between my legs, I apologized to the vet and told her what happened. I was fooled by my dog's acting. And for this trick, why not give her a bite of steak? And so I did. From that moment on, she knew she had me. I would do anything to get her to eat.

Her acting and her beauty never faded. Her big brown eyes were so completely expressive that you could always see the bubble above her head and knew what it said. She was just that expressive. The poor thing always had a camera or phone in her face. And she never wanted her pictures taken. The minute you got a great photo lined up, she would look away. I lost great photo opportunities because she decided it was unnecessary to document her beauty or her acting. For Natty, it was a clear case of, 'to know her is to love her.' And she was convinced that the only way to know her was to be in her presence. She wanted to charm you in person rather than to just show off. It was as if she was saying, "No paparazzi... no, really, NO paparazzi!"

She was such a character that I could have had her cast as an actor pup. But she was content to just be. I think she was trying to tell me to also be in the moment and enjoy it for what it was and to put the camera down. The moment is fleeting. It would pass, long before I could click the camera icon on my phone. In the end, I think I got a few great shots of her that showed her loving soul, her beauty, and even some of her antics. But for the most part, I just enjoyed and loved watching her acting expertise.

Natty the Protector

Divorce is never easy; not for the ones in the relationship, nor for their loved ones. Sometimes, it is easier to just stay in the relationship. The mere thought of breaking the news to the ones you love will rip you to shreds. It will break your heart until you just stay one more hour, day or week. And then you will be reminded why you need to leave. He will yell, scream, or throw something. Or... worse.

And Natty would hide under the table when he screamed. I thought she was just a skittish little puppy. She never acted scared around his cat that was three times her size. She held her own with the cat when he swatted her for stealing his food. Then she stayed clear of him. It was fine. She figured it out. She didn't hide or shy away from him.

But when the human him would yell, she would hide. Maybe it was loud noises? Because really anytime he yelled or slammed a door, she went for cover like she was a trained kid from California. Duck and run for cover under a table or doorway as soon as you feel the earth move. Was this her earth moving? Or was it mine? For me, this was an earth-shattering relationship. I did not know how to handle the yelling, throwing, or banging. I wanted to run for cover too.

And that is when I realized it: she was afraid of him. And to protect her, I had to leave him. Yes, let me say that again. To protect *her*, I had to leave him. He crossed so many lines, I couldn't find my boundaries anymore. It was Natty that told me he was scary and I needed to run from him. Get protection. Get away. So, I did – I ran for cover.

He moved out. He left the boy cat. And then Natty really came alive. Truly alive. She figured this was her family and her house. And she found her bark. With the big him gone, and her new bark established, she decided it was time to take her position as the ruler. So, if the cat decided to scratch the furniture, she put him in his place. It is not that she barked a lot, but she made it clear that she was allowed on the furniture and he wasn't even allowed to touch, much less scratch it. Maybe he was afraid she would bark and not stop. Maybe he thought she would jump on his back and stay there. Who knows?

Soon it wasn't just the cat and the furniture. Soon, it was the whole house she managed. She would look out the big picture window that overlooked the driveway.

Lessons Learned from My Rescue Dog

If someone she did not know crossed the driveway she would make her presence known. Again, she was a tiny little six-pound dog looking out the window that conservatively measured 4 x 6 feet. She looked like a tiny little mouse looking out that window. But somehow everyone knew she owned the house.

I will never know how she figured out he left for good. After all, it wasn't the first time he had left. But somehow, she just knew. She was truly that smart. And now that she owned the cat and the house, it was my turn. She set about training me. Meals were the first item on her agenda.

Weaning her off of the home cooked meals was the first trick. She wanted human food for sure, but she no longer wanted boiled chicken and rice. She wanted steak and potatoes. She did not want eggs unless it was an omelet with veggies and cheese. And she wouldn't eat until she got what she wanted. And soon, she owned me.

Telling Natty that we were getting a divorce was easy. Turns out it was just as easy to tell everyone in my life. They all loved me and they all understood and were honestly relieved for me. But Natty – she knew more. She knew he was just the wrong guy. And any guy I met after, she made her feelings known. Not in a sweet sort of way. She was more petulant. She would either bark her head off at the guy, or would simply turn her nose up at him and then go to her bedroom.

Eventually, I met the right guy. The really right guy. The one I was ready to introduce to Natty. And the day that she met Glenn, she sniffed him and went to his lap! I swear the bubble above her head said, "Finally! You finally found him!" And as I recall, Glenn gave me grief for warning him that she could be picky. Every meal I made that she did not eat, she would eat it from Glenn. This was her way of telling me that this was the guy who could feed her. Yes, she ruled the house. And she picked her family.

Natty the Healer

They say when you are sad, lonely, depressed, in mourning, and even sick – all you really need is someone to stand with you in that feeling. You just want to be heard, to know that you are not alone.

When I was sick, I would just want to crawl into bed and not move. When I was sad... really immobile with depression, I would either be stuck on the couch with some mindless tv show on or hiding under the covers. I would just blankly watch the screen hoping beyond hope that I would at least start to imagine myself as a character in the show. In the comedies, it was a lighter version of life. When it was a drama on, at least the show ended and usually the issue was resolved in an hour. And so, it provided hope that my issue would resolve.

In the meantime, I just wanted to stop feeling alone in my misery. I didn't necessarily want to know that anyone else had gone through my horrors, I just wanted to have company. The days I couldn't get up, Natty would lay down with me. And I knew I was not alone. She was the soul that would lay by my side – no matter whether it was the couch or the bed, she would not move until I moved. No matter where I was, she glued herself to my side. She was standing, or laying as it were, in comfort and solidarity with me. I think for her, like most animals, she was empathetic and knew when I needed comfort. It is almost as if she took it on as her duty and honor to be there for me. Like she knew just lying by my side would make me feel better. I would eventually get up if she lay with me long enough. And truly, she was never wrong.

I realized she was a truly special soul when I saw her do this with others. It was one thing that she did it with me. After all, I was her human. We were connected; bonded. But with anyone who needed healing, she was there. Even if she did not know the person – if they entered our house sick, she was there.

I had a cousin visit us. She was in transit to a smaller town and stopped by for a visit. It turned out she was running a 103 fever and was really sick. And there was a freak ice storm in Atlanta. She was going nowhere. So, I got her to lie down on the couch in the living room and I made her tea, gave her medicine, and took care of her.

Natty took one look at her when she first walked into the house and knew she had a job to do. So, she started to hang out with her. She tried to sneak into her room at night to sleep with her. Because the door was closed, she ended up visiting her room three times in the middle of the night to sniff wildly at the door. There were no lights, no sounds... just Natty's concern. I turned out, she was just trying to make sure my cousin was ok. Each time she got up, we got up. We finally realized Natty was just checking in on my cousin.

The next morning when she came downstairs, Natty followed and climbed on her so that she would not move. Well, at least Natty thought she could not move if she was on her; never mind that Natty is all of six pounds to the adult human size my cousin is. Yet, Natty stayed there for two full days until my cousin's fever broke. And that was that. After that, Natty couldn't be bothered with her. She came back to us to hang out. It is the acknowledgement of an issue and the solidarity that Natty offered to anyone in need that made my heart melt.

There is a cat who lives in a hospice care facility. This cat will go and sleep with anyone who is about to pass within the next 48 hours. He is said to be so accurate that the nurses will call the family as soon as they see the cat go into the person's room. It seems almost creepy to know your time is up if an animal visits with you. Maybe it is cool. The cat is sharing its knowledge with you and you have a chance to say goodbye. Natty was different... she literally nursed people back to health. Natty had a heart as soft as a pillow, and just wanted to ake care of everyone. It was her honor and duty. It was the role she played. She was a sweet, loving soul who took care of people when they were in need. With all of her heart, she knew her love could help. And so she did.

Natty Accepts All Creatures

Whenever we run into a person who handles a given situation differently than we would, my husband likes to say, "It takes all kinds." It is his way of expressing his acceptance of all people. After all, we come from different places and have different ideas. We all have differences of opinions. It is our differences that make us unique and keep life interesting.

As young children, we find comfort in doing the same thing as our classmates. We take solace in it. And God forbid we are even a little different, we get utterly distressed. We just want to have the same type of birthday party as Tommy or do our hair the same as Jane. Then we get a little older... enter our mid to late teens and we start to explore our differences. We desperately want to stand out... to be unique. The funny thing for onlookers is that those differences that we are celebrating are most likely the same as every other person. Because at heart, we are all souls looking to connect, love, and be loved. And when we celebrate the differences we seem to have, we become a better society. When we connect with one another, talk to each other about our experiences and our differences, we learn that at the heart of it, there is something familiar in all of it. There is something we can relate to. There is something there that makes us the same... uniquely the same; and every last one of us deserving of acceptance and love.

This is something Natty knew inherently. When I adopted her, she acquired a cat-brother. She accepted him immediately as one of our pack. Never in her time with him did she ever treat him like anything other than a sibling and another soul who was as entitled as she to be in the house. She knew there were different rules for both of them, but she also knew he was family. He could have normal canned food, but she had to be on a special diet, and could not eat his food. She tried to eat his food once, and he gave her three swift slaps to the face. And just like that, she listened to his opinion of sharing his food, and respected the distance. She never tried to eat his food again. Of course, she also made him listen to me about not scratching the new furniture. She could go on the sofa, but he could not scratch it. And boy did she take it upon herself to enforce that rule. Natty was a unique soul in that it took thirty minutes for her to accept Bowzer as her brother. She learned to live with him and even love him. And of course, boss him around.

A while later, and after Bowzer had passed away, Kaari moved in. She also had a cat, Mr. Underfoot.

Lessons Learned from My Rescue Dog

Mr. U was about three times the size of Natty and not particularly impressed with Natty as a dog. Natty couldn't really be bothered with him either, except to know that he was a family member. And as such she assumed it was cool to be in his face. Size was irrelevant to her. I am not sure how the actual circumstances came to pass as we were at work, but one day we got home to find Natty freshly washed by our cleaning lady. This was definitely above and beyond the call of duty. So when I asked what inspired the deed, she told us that when she was cleaning Kaari's room, she found them both curled up under the bed. When Natty came out to greet her, there was a long pee line running from the nape of her neck to her tail. Mr. U had marked her and she accepted it as his seal of approval of her. After that, there was peace between these two souls. They accepted everything about each other. She had said her piece, he said his, and they lived together and loved one another.

After Mr. U and his mom moved away, I decided it was time for another playmate for Natty. It is not that she ever acted like a dog or even gave a hint that she wanted to add any more to our "pack." But something told me it was time to have another soul in our house. After all, Natty was getting older, and I was starting to truly fear losing her. I had no clue how I would handle not having her around. She was not just a dog to me, she was part of my heart. At ten years old, she was officially a senior dog. I knew her life span could be another ten years. But the reality is, she was sickly when I got her, and still small and finicky with her food. She was even starting to get set in her ways. After doing some research and talking to some friends, I realized now was the time to get a new dog. Natty would help me train the new one, and some of Natty's personality might even rub off on the new soul. I was also hoping a younger dog would help to get Natty a little more active and maybe even make her feel younger.

And so, we went in search of another puppy. We (I took Natty with me) looked at many rescues. We tried to walk them, we tried to sit with them, we tried to just be in their space. They were either too overpowering or too rambunctious, and one was even a bit mean to Natty – nipping and snapping at her. And then we met Dolly. She was a puppy. A bit rambunctious, but not overly so. She let Natty be the alpha, and they were both able to sit in my lap for 15 minutes. We found our puppy and brought her home.

Dolly was our Valentine's Day gift. Natty took it upon herself to house train Dolly and teach her the ways of the house. Dolly would chew everything in sight, would break free from her crate, and would generally make a mess. But just like Natty saved the new couch from Bowzer, she taught Dolly how to be a dog. Somehow she still let Dolly be Dolly though.

Lessons Learned from My Rescue Dog

Dolly would zip around and run in the yard, and Natty would just patiently watch her. Often, I would get the look from Natty that asked me why exactly we needed a dog in our lives… but then she would snuggle up to Dolly and fall asleep. No matter their differences, Natty loved Dolly.

And later, when Emma the Purr - our new kitten - came into the picture, Natty even taught Dolly the loving tolerance of all animals in this house. She taught Dolly to love Emma. She protected Emma from Dolly's growls and barks until eventually Dolly learned Emma is family. She is one to cuddle with. She is one to love. And even now, Emma is Dolly's best buddy. They kiss and cuddle all the time.

This absolute acceptance of all creatures young, old, big, small, cat or dog was one of the sweetest lessons I have ever learned from Ms. Natty. She accepted all creatures and taught us all the meaning of love and acceptance.

Natty and her Wanderlust

There are those who have the wanderlust… those who must travel because there is no other option but to go out and explore. They must go touch, see, feel and explore new places. It does not matter if the place is far away, or just up the street, the fact is a soul afflicted with wanderlust must explore; find new things to see and experience. As someone afflicted with wanderlust, I attribute this to having a zest for and a love of life and living life; for I too just need to explore my world.

Ms. Natty also loved to explore. I've told you about how she sniffed every inch of the small dog area at the park. Well, she did this same type of sniffing in her own yard. She would smell everything so intently and then after a rain, she would do it all over again. Even on walks, she had to smell every new street we walked on so thoroughly that she knew everything. It was this intense investigating that she did on her street that allowed her to know instinctively that we were coming up on our street. I could never get her to pass by for a longer walk – we had to figure out other routes. Before I moved her into my new place, I shored up the perimeter with chicken wire so she couldn't get to the neighbor's yard. But one day, she was able to dig around it and went off to smell the neighbor's yards. When it started happening more often, I would find her 1 or 2 blocks away.

And no matter how much she liked to escape her own yard and wander afar, for some reason when I took her hiking in the mountains and let her off leash, she knew enough to stay within earshot of me. I am not sure how I figured this out... but somehow, she stayed close in when hiking. Maybe it was because she thought I needed the protection. Or maybe she was letting me join her on her wander. Because really, she loved to wander. In the mountains, if I whistled, she would appear instantly. She absolutely loved hiking with me and would love to just smell everything. After a few off leash hikes I realized that she was not escaping for any other reason than to savor everything she could. She just wanted to take it all in, learn everything she could about her environment and savor every moment.

I believe she just wanted to be outside. She just wanted to explore and be in the world. She wanted to be an active participant of it all. As she grew older and more feeble, she still adored her walks. She absolutely loved going even though it caused her pain. In the end, we would carry her while we walked Dolly. And she was so happy to just be a part of the exploration.

Lessons Learned from My Rescue Dog

Seeing her enjoy in the way that she could, even if that meant being carried, reminded me how important it is to savor our moments. Enjoy our lives, explore and to get a little lost in our wanderings.

All too often, as we get older, we slow down. I met a lady recently in her late 70's. She said she was motivated by her doctor to move. Apparently, her doctor gave her some sage advice. He said that your 20's prepare you for your 30's, your 30's for your 40's, and so on. So if you move in your 20's you move more in your 30's your 30's for your 40's, and so on. Natty embodied this. She moved. All the time. And when she couldn't move she took help and still wandered. If only we can all be the object that stays in motion.

Natty Doesn't Play Fetch

It was an exciting, busy morning. I was getting married to the man of my dreams! I had a house full of people, some getting dressed, some fussing over me, some staying out of the way. My lovely fiancé came over with his family to say hi and to see the puppies. His nephew was particularly interested in meeting them. He wanted his own puppy and figured his favorite uncle and these little pups could help him convince his parents that they too needed a puppy. He even brought toys for them. Toys he had paid for himself. They were cute squeaky teddy bears.

Rahul was so excited to give the toys, but wanted to show me first. He was so sweet about it, that I almost did not say anything. But then, I figured I had to. I told him, that it was such a sweet thing he had done that I would remember and cherish it as one of my favorite stories from my wedding day. I continued to explain that while Dolly may in fact play with the toys, Natty would never. She simply did not consider herself a dog.

Dear Rahul did not take this as a word of caution, rather as a challenge. He sincerely thought in the 30 minutes we had left before we departed for the ceremony, that he could teach Natty to play fetch. I giggled to myself, but was secretly appreciative of the time it would give me to put the final touches on my makeup and hair. I saw that he threw the first toy, and Dolly went running to it, planted herself and just squeaked the heck out of her toy. They tell me that he then threw it for Natty. She gave him her best contemptuous stare as if to say, "Now, why would you do that?" When he said fetch, she continued to look at him as if to say, "You threw it, you go get it!" And as if he heard her, he skipped over to it, and brought it back to her. This scene apparently repeated a few times, until Glenn quipped, "Well Rahul, it looks like Natty taught you how to fetch!"

I wasn't there for the fetching, but I knew Natty well enough that I knew every look she gave him. And I knew that no matter how many times the scene repeated, it would have stayed the same. To know Natty was to love her, and to want to play with her. She just believed she was above the games of dogs. She believed so strongly that she was a princess, that even when playing fetch, the human doing the tossing would also do the fetching. All she need do was to watch and offer a dismissive stare. And so it was. That is the only way she ever played fetch. She watched the toy get tossed, and then watch the person tossing the toy fetch it and do it again. She believed it so much, acted accordingly, and so it was.

Natty never did something simply because it was expected of her. I don't think I have ever been so steadfast in the belief of anything… even about myself. I wonder if I'd had strong beliefs in myself if I would ever have been disappointed. Ever had heartbreak. That level of belief takes courage, strength, dedication and pure love of self. To have this love and respect for yourself can take you far in life. To live in love of others and yourself is what Natty did. And what she taught me to do. I will remember to believe in myself. I will remember to honor my desires and not to jump simply because someone entices and beckons me.

Now, if I were a dog… but like Natty, I am not.

Natty Shared Her Food

As I've said, Natty was a foodie. I know, most dogs eat anything. Heck, Georgie, my cat, will eat anything you give him. It's kind of hysterical watching him go after the salad on your plate or even to watch him eat popcorn. But I digress. I was telling you about Natty... she absolutely loved good food. She also absolutely loved pizza, cheap hamburgers, filet mignon, Indian food, Chinese food, Mexican food, and bread. That girl just loved good food... and burgers. I have no idea how in one day, her palate could go from filet mignon to a fast food hamburger, but it could. That is not to say she didn't also like the finer burgers out there... it was just that some weird thing went off in her head if she smelled it.

If food came in the form of dog food, she would maybe... maybe eat it a few times, pick at it a little, and in her own way demand that she get something different. I can't blame her. I would not want to eat the same thing every meal. She wanted variety. I understood that. I am not one for leftovers. Especially 3 days in a row. So, how could I blame my Natty girl?

So, we got into a routine of giving her what she needed and mixing a teaspoon or so of something special into it. But when we got Dolly, we were anxious to make her feedings as easy as possible. And lo and behold, Dolly was a dog's dog. Dolly would happily eat anything set before her. I could feed her the same dog food every day and she'd be happy as a clam. Of course, she realized Natty was getting something special. Or maybe she didn't. Dolly was also a rescue. She was a stray roaming the Kern county streets of California when she was picked up at a year old. She was also underweight and was just glad when food was around.

So, even if there was no food left in Natty's bowl, Dolly would obsessively lick it. I was not sure if she was just trying to get the flavor essence or if she actually thought food particles remained when there was clearly nothing. In any case, when Natty realized that this was Dolly's compulsion, she started to leave a bite in the bowl for Dolly. Unless of course, it was filet mignon; in that case, Natty left nothing. But everything else, Natty would leave a bite. And Dolly was so grateful. It was the sweetest thing to see my little angel do something so loving for her sister whom she found so completely annoying.

Dolly also overate... well, was overfed. She too started off underweight and at her most was three pounds over what she should have been. For a dog that is supposed to be fifteen pounds, that is a lot. When we first put her on her diet was when we started to see that Natty was not just leaving morsels behind for Dolly to lick up, but actually leaving bites behind. It was as if she knew Dolly was hungry. And she knew that hunger could only be filled with shared bites from her. Maybe that is why Natty did not need to eat as much... because I was willing to share what was on my plate with her. And she knew that was needed to solve the hunger: the shared plate. It was so heartwarming to see Natty share her plate. We actually added extra bites into Natty's bowl so that she did not lose more weight. But of course, she somehow knew and just ended up leaving more food for Dolly. In order to sustain Dolly's weight loss, we just let her have the extra bites from Natty and walked her more. To this day, my husband and I eat nearly every meal as if it were Tapas. We share everything - whether we trade plates half way through or just eat off one plate. We love to do it. It never really occurred to me before that we learned this from Natty but there you have it. We love to share our plates. Even in the fanciest of restaurants. It just tastes better. It is yet another lesson from Natty... and another way to honor her.

Natty's love and care really showed months after Natty passed - when we got Georgie. While Dolly was not in love with him, she started to leave her precious bites behind for him. Because just like she did with Natty, George would lick Dolly's bowl after she was done. And Dolly learned from Natty to share her food

Natty Shared Her Food

To share her abundance. Because she saw when Natty shared, her hunger subsided. And when Dolly shared, Dolly got more food. While neither Dolly nor Emma have quite taken to Georgie as fast as they took to each other, they know he is one of us. They love him and take care of him. We are one. The more we share the more we have to share.

Natty Radar

Remember when you were a kid who got just a little taste of freedom? Your mom or dad would always want to know where you were going, what you were going to do when you got there, and when you would be back. It was so annoying. And then you got your cell phone; it was all about texting when you got somewhere and always keeping in touch.

As a parent you were glad to have the GPS tracker on your kid's phone so you always knew where your kid was. As the parent, you always wanted to make sure your kid was safe. There is something just innate and overwhelming and you just need to know your kid is safe. And it is all the better when they are in the house, better yet when they are within earshot. It is not that you want to stifle your children or their freedom; you just want to know they are safe. You're not intending to be overprotective; you just needed to know. And when something goes awry, your radar goes off. There could be a marching band playing in your house and if your kid cries, you hear it above all else. This is when you realize you have radar hearing for your child.

Natty Radar

As I write this, I realize this story has changed. I intended to write about me having some innate sense for Natty. I always thought I knew when something was wrong with her and how to help her make it better. I knew when she liked someone, when she tolerated someone, and when she would do anything to stay away from someone. I always took it as my duty to watch over and protect her and her space. But what I realize is that even in her sleep, she was the one with the radar... radar ears. She would be curled up, seemingly asleep, and then her ears would stand straight up. Her left ear would stay perked up while the other would rotate around listening for me. And so, it appears that Ms. Natty thought she was my mum. She thought she had to keep an ear out for me and make sure I was ok. It was Natty who took it as her responsibility to watch out for me, listen for me, and guide my life. Some say your mama knows best. But for me, it was Natty. Natty knew best. As evidenced by Natty's pick of Glenn.

Natty stopped radar-ing as much when Glenn came into the picture. It was as if she knew that I was now taken care of and she could relax. Of course when he went out of town the first time, she had a fit. She sat attentively on the edge of the bed staring at the door waiting for him to return. When he did return two weeks later, she threw a full-blown temper tantrum. She would wake him up every 15 minutes to make sure he was cuddling her. After that, we all took to calling her Glenn's girlfriend. We thought she had a crush on him… but maybe she just knew that he needed to be in the house, not outside of it. It was yet another example of Natty knowing and taking care of me.

When she got comfortable with Glenn being around she finally did the Chihuahua thing of burrowing under the covers at night. And even during the day, her radar ears subsided. Though later in life, as her hearing started to go, she relied on her eyesight. She would chase us down from whatever room we were in and lead us to the bedroom. She figured if she couldn't hear us, at least she could see us. At least that way she knew we were under her watchful eye and nothing could go wrong. And if something did go wrong, she would be there to make it all better. After all, any parent just wants to protect her children and know that they are ok.

And so it goes. This is yet another lesson from my beloved rescue dog. She taught me that time is an elusive thing. You cannot get it back. You must savor your moments with your loved ones. Keep them safe. Keep them near. Love them and protect them.

Don't Worry Until You Have To

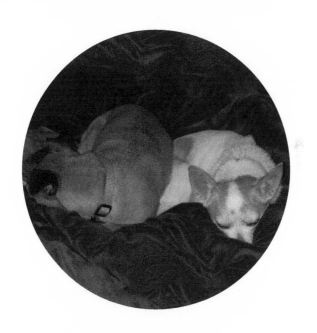

So, I am sitting in the waiting room of the big, fancy-do-everything animal hospital for another ultrasound. This time it is for Dolly. But it is all too reminiscent of when I sat here waiting for Ms. Natty. With Ms. Natty, I was here waiting to find out what the growth on her back really was. We found out it was cancer. And we could have operated, but then there was the issue with her heart and kidneys. So, we decided not to do anything.

Is that what an act of mercy is? To just let her live her days without invasive surgeries? We were in an impossible situation. While the surgery could be effective, the medicines would ruin her kidneys even more. And if we tried to fix her kidneys, those meds would hurt her heart. (Big sigh.) What is the more merciful choice?

And while we were learning this about Natty, we found out Dolly had cancer in her toe. What?! I thought I was being smart getting my babies so far apart in age. That way they wouldn't leave me at that same time. What wicked, twisted sense of fate was this? All in the same week. In the end, Dolly survived. And Natty lived to see at least that much.

I am nothing if not diligent about Dolly's health. She always gets chews to help keep her teeth cleaned. She even gets dental cleanings every year. I learned this lesson with Natty. Keep your teeth clean and healthy as they are the gateway to the rest of your body. When I first got Natty, she was so sickly that she vomited all the time. It turned out her liver enzymes were extremely elevated. Once we got her teeth cleaned up, her kidneys or her liver – or whatever was causing the enzymes to be elevated – finally cleared too. Eventually, as she aged, the liver enzyme issue came back, signaling her kidneys were starting to go. It was years before they actually failed. But we took care of her as best we could along the way – Denamarin, teeth cleaning, etc. etc. The big take-away was to take ownership of health. So, I took ownership of my babies' health. I was almost aggressive in preventative care for them. And yet, when it came to the tougher issues… like the surgery or no for Natty, I couldn't do it. Was it more merciful for her? Or more so for me?

After we learned of Natty's issue, we had a good 4 months. They had said she had 3-6 months. And we saw the decline happening with her – even before her diagnoses. So, when Dolly's liver enzyme issues started, it was no big deal. It was just a little elevated. So, she went on Denamarin, a diet, and we upped her exercise a bit. And it was fine… until the following year when the numbers went up a little again. And then the following year it went up yet again. So, the vet decided it was time to test the bile acids. Thankfully, Dolly got an overall clean bill of health. But still, the enzyme worry persisted. And it was elevated enough to get tested.

So, now I find myself sitting in the waiting room again. This time for Dolly. Though this time is a bit different. There was no clear decline in Dolly's behavior. She is of course a little sleepier than when she was younger. But we walk so much further now than we used to, doesn't that help? OK, enough of the mental seesaw. As with Natty, we would just take any results when they come. And we would make the plan after the news. I knew there was no use in worry. We would just have to wait to hear. What, put worry aside? I know, it is a ground-breaking idea. But I was determined just write this story instead of worrying about the appointment. I had spent so many days weeks and months worrying about Natty. I knew I had to learn to leave worry behind. Worry would only rob me of the joy of the moment. So, I sat there watching Dolly be social with the boy dogs and the humans. It was actually sweet. I loved watching her. And writing this story.

And so, our name was finally called and I was allowed to go in! The doctor doing the ultra sound was surprised that we were there at all; and yet he understood the precautions given her age. I got to pet her as the ultra sound went on. I swear I felt the shock of the cool liquid as it was squirted on Dolly's tummy. The doctor just kept showing me fuzzy picture after fuzzy picture. I think he knew how scared I was. He just kept talking about Dolly's dress or how sweet she was. And then he told me the sweetest news I could ever hope to hear. He said, "Normally, with a dog this age, I'd see something, but there is absolutely nothing to see. She is incredibly healthy. Nothing to worry about." Whew. Yay for no worrying before time; no planning before necessary. Just breathe, take precautions, listen to the doctor. Exercise. And keep your teeth clean.

Natty Taught Me About Unconditional Love

know I did not pick Natty. I know she picked me. And I like to think that Natty picked Dolly. But I wonder if Dolly didn't have more to do with the picking and Natty did the agreeing. We had seen many other puppies that were just lovely and some would have likely been smaller than Dolly. But that did not matter to her. In the end, Dolly was the only one who was calm and subservient enough that Natty knew she could teach Dolly how to behave. And truly, when I sat down, Dolly just squirmed her way into my lap right beside Natty.

And then she squirmed her way into our hearts. Now, I cannot think of her as anything but my teddy bear, my buddy, and my puppy love. Or maybe it was Natty who felt her vibration and decided that she would allow her to share my lap. In this way, Natty taught me about having my guard up and how and when to let it down. She taught me when to be open, when to trust, and when to let go. I suppose that is the purpose of pets for young children. They are there to teach children about unconditional love (the love they share with the animal) and death.

Natty Taught Me About Unconditional Love

I like to think that I picked Glenn. Or at the very least, that I manifested him as my life partner... I determined what I wanted in the perfect man... in the perfect relationship. I wrote it out in a list... that list was so long, it actually told a story of how I wished my life to be. Then, I put the list aside and joined a dating website. Eventually, it was he who contacted me. And it was how much Natty instantly loved him that made me fall in love with him more. So, it could have been him that picked me, or her that made me fall in love with him, or some cosmic force that made my wish list come true and brought us all together.

In any case, trusting, receiving, and loving were all things Natty taught me in my darkest days. When I was living through some of the hardest times I have ever experienced, she was there to trust that I would always take care of her. She was there to love me and let me love her. At times she was more patient than I was with transforming Dolly into being a house dog rather than a mutt living on the street. And when she grew to love a friend that suddenly moved, or left the house, she would welcome them back with an open heart as soon as they returned - even if it was months later.

Natty knew how to love. And she knew how to let go. She knew that when someone was sad or sick, sometimes the best thing to do was to sit by his or her side and offer her comfort. And so when the doctors said she had a mass and that there was nothing to do because surgery was too risky for her enlarged heart and the meds would put her failing kidneys at risk, all that was left to do was to be with her. Sit by her and offer her comfort and love. This is when she most loved having all of us… Glenn, me, dog, and kitten on the bed with her. This is when we indulged her the most. It was the least we could do. After all of the heart aches, the colds, the surgeries she sat through with us, this was the least we could do.

When I first found out that she had cancer and it was basically inoperable, I told her I loved her and that I was ready to let her go. I just wanted her to not suffer. I think Glenn had the harder time with it. She just wasn't getting better. And soon her decline was too much to ignore. When it got too much to bear when she coughed more than she slept, we decided to put her down on Saturday. It was Thursday evening. It was like she knew what we were saying. It was like she understood that her time had come and we were both ready to let her go. She had one more fitful night. It was so bad even Dolly and Emma stayed up all night. And we knew even one more day would be too much. It would be cruel. We decided to take her in on Friday morning. It was the right decision at the right time.

So we took her into the vet she knew… and they treated us like Royalty. I always expected that any vet would treat a family going through this situation well, but what I did not expect was how many people wanted to say goodbye to her. They took her in the back, and everyone came out crying to offer their sympathies. For a moment, I almost thought that I was spending more time consoling them than the other way around. But then I realized just how many people's lives Ms. Natty touched. She was truly beloved. Even in her crankiest days, she was adored by so many. And that actually made my heart lighter. It made me feel good to know that she would live on in the love she shared.

They offered many options for her ashes. There are companies that will actually make jewelry out of ashes. They offered garden stones. They offered an urn… but in the end, I couldn't get any of them. Wearing her, seeing her in the garden, or even on the mantel could not make me remember her more. It all felt like I would just reduce her to a thing to be owned. She was bigger than that. For some, it is the right choice, the right ritual to have something to remember their loved ones. But I just wanted to set all of her free. Free from her obligations and the body that was tormenting her. And goodness forbid if that item ever got lost or broke; it would be like losing her all over again. I just could not lose her again. Without capturing her in a thing… it felt like letting her go… letting her be free. After all, she would never be far from our thoughts or hearts.

Lessons Learned from My Rescue Dog

In the end, we chose a ritual… we went to the beach and let her go in the surf. She became part of the big blue ocean. And now, any time I think of or look at the ocean, I see her. For she is ruling that world now.

Natty – Hugs and Loves

I am a hugger. A big, throw my arms out and wrap as much of you in them as I can hugger. My favorite hugs are with people who respond and we end up heart to heart, holding our hearts in from the back as we embrace. At the end of the day, if we live with love, it is our hearts that speak to one another. I have learned to live with those who do not respond, who give the side hug, who are not ready for the let it all hang out hug. I get that. Maybe we don't know each other that well, and our hug represents that. Or maybe we need that big hug even more. There is a Hindu spiritual leader called Ammaji (which means "mom"), known far and wide. She is so popular, she will actually travel around the world to bestow her hugs. People will come to her and give her a wish or tell her their troubles and she will bless you and give you a hug. I have had the good fortune to receive her blessings and hugs twice, the first in 1999 and the second in 2009. She will give hugs and chocolate kisses to you.

In the late 2000's the "Free Hugs" Movement started and people are recruited all over the world to give free hugs to anyone passing by. It warms my heart that people understand how vital hugs are. How imperative they are for our society. Do you remember when you were a kid and you had a fight with your friend? Once it was resolved, your mom or your teacher always said, "OK, hug now. You are friends." Hugs are vital. It always warms my heart to see people giving out free hugs. I always take one when I can. And why not? Getting one is also about giving one. And that is the best circle of love. In the end, it is our hearts touching. Because there is so much life and love in our touch. We know this to be scientific fact: the more we touch, the better. We physically need to touch and be touched. Even Natty knew touch was vital.

While she was not a fan of the full hug, Natty definitely knew that touch was as important to her as the receiver as it was to me the provider. As a younger dog, she loved having her chest rubbed. She would look at you, and just lift one paw and that was the invitation to rub her chest. I used to think she liked her belly rubbed, but then I realized, it was in fact her chest. It was her version of giving and receiving from her heart. And goodness knows if you stopped before she was ready, then she would let you know… she would snuggle up to you, jump on your lap, roll half way over, head cocked upside down, or just paw at your hand until you continued caressing her heart. We all laughed at seeing this six-pound little girl contort herself just to be touched in the exact way she wanted. This was more proof, not that we needed it, that she was a determined little girl.

As her arthritis in her back worsened, she had less and less ability to sit on her hind legs and raise her front paw. So she stopped raising her paw. But by then we were so conditioned to rubbing her chest, that when she was lying on her side, it was an automatic thing for those that knew her well. The only other place she loved as much was being scratched on her neck, just under her collar. Soon after we got her little sister, Dolly, the two would fall asleep with Natty touching Dolly. But as her hearing went, she got closer and closer; I often found them cuddling together.

It did not dawn on me at the time, but Natty was not just touching Dolly for the security of trusting her ears, but Natty was also touching Dolly and passing the torch, as it were. Later, we got Emma, our cat. Even Emma knew Natty needed to be touched. She would often reach out to Natty to just touch her. She would simply rest the tip of her paw on Natty's back as if to say, "I'm here. I've got your back." At first I thought Emma was checking to see if she was alive, but later I realized it was to tell Natty that she was not alone. We think Emma knew Natty was fatally ill. At first, Natty would not let Emma touch her, but as she got sicker she not only allowed it; she would sit near Emma so that she could reach her. That is when we knew Natty was beyond anything we could do for her. We did take her to the vet, and found out because of all the different complications there wasn't a thing we could do for her. All that was left was to bring her home and love her for as much time as we had left.

All we could do was touch her to show her our love. And so we did… and when we couldn't, Dolly and Emma touched her. One or another would be curled up next to Natty. I always knew touch and hugging were important, but seeing how long Natty survived with touch alone was eye-opening. The night before Natty died was a particularly hard one for her. She was up most of the night coughing and trying to breathe or just be comfortable. Dolly and Emma never left her side. When we came home without her, they were fine. They seemed to know that it was her time. And they continued to take their afternoon and evening sleeps together.

Several months later, we brought home a new kitten, George. It was a mere two weeks that took Emma from hissing skepticism to Emma and George sleeping paw to paw. Whether asleep or awake, touch is vital. It invites you into the inner sanctum of someone's space and life.

Lessons Learned from My Rescue Dog

As it happened, I went to a conference where I met many wonderful people. One of these people traveled the world hugging people. And another one espoused love so much that everything she made was covered in the word. Feeling the love and warmth from these two was overwhelming. And it made me realize that these were the same messages from my Natty girl. When she loved someone, she hugged and loved without reserve. And when she needed hugs and love, she was fearless in demanding them. I will be forever grateful to these lessons I learned from Natty. She taught me to trust, hug, and love big.

But as her hearing went, she got closer and closer. I often found them cuddling together. Later, I came across various articles and studies that proved just how smart Ms. Natty was. All of these studies reported that there was much to be gained by holding hands and hugging. There are actual medical benefits to touch, including reducing stress and having a happier and longer life. Hmmm… the things that little dog knew. And she never even learned to read!

Natty Passes the Baton

have told you the story how Natty ruled our house; how she trained Dolly; how she picked Glenn; how she trained Dolly to not just like, but love Emma. But what I have not talked about… in fact, what I did not even notice until recently was that Natty actually passed the baton to Emma.

Oh sure, we all knew Emma is extremely intelligent. More than that, she is incredibly compassionate. Whenever Natty was not well, Emma would reach out and touch Natty. She would watch over Natty; she would reach out and touch her as she slept. She would follow her around to make sure she was ok and did not have any mistakes around the house. It was the most endearing thing in the world to see Emma shower affection and still let Natty feel like she had her space and maintained her place on the top. The balance they struck was amazing.

Then Natty passed away. And the girls just knew. We took her out in the morning, and they never expected her back. They never looked for her. They just knew. But her absence left a deafening silence. Dolly and Emma were happy and cuddly, and subdued. Time marched on, and Emma and Dolly just went about life. When we brought George home, Emma was less than thrilled. She was mortified.

I am still not sure if it is because George is a boy, or if he was just needy and adorably clueless. Or maybe it is a beautiful combination of his complete gorgeousness combined with his complete lack of savvy. I mean really, how many cats do you know who had to be taught to clean themselves?? Yup, Emma had to teach the little boy how to clean himself. For the longest time, we would watch him clean himself and would literally stop in our tracks to watch in wonder at how he has advanced. He was so helpless and you just had to love him for it. Or in Emma's case, she chose to look down her perfectly elegant pink nose at this fluffy mess of a child. Even so, she took to cleaning him constantly. He still has not figured out how to use the litter box without stepping in his own pee and tracking it out. It wasn't just the juxtaposition of his cluelessness to Emma's complete regality. It was also that he had so much more energy than Emma ever showed. All of that energy was a bit much for poor Emma. Though in time, she learned to play with him… make him run and then take a sudden turn and watch as he just looked befuddled. Eventually, Emma did take to George. She started to take care of him and even groom him.

Lessons Learned from My Rescue Dog

What we did not immediately realize was that as time passed, she not only took over as caretaker and guardian, but she also took over Natty's favorite spots. Natty liked to perch on the highest spot available. If that meant she would need to knock over a pillow or cushion to sit on top of it, she would. Just like the royal being she was. Eventually, Emma did this too. She took over Natty's favorite cushion. I would wake up, and she would be sitting on the bedside table or the mantel watching over her realm.

Emma took over other things too. Whenever we go out of town for an extended period of time, we leave the cats with the vet. And Emma, who used to be quiet, now chats with us in the car - just as Natty used to do. In everything she has taken over, the biggest thing she took over was taking care of us.

Whenever Glenn and I would have an animated discussion, be it some minor misunderstanding or frustration about someone or something else, Natty would always come and sit by one of our sides. And now, Emma will come sit by me. More than that, Emma will actually come and try to kiss me - especially when I am upset. Is it possible that Emma is smarter than Natty? Emma has learned to wake us up by sniffing our lips. We call it kissing because, well, it is just cute. She has observed Glenn and me kissing every morning to wake each other up and often during the day. She has figured out that this is the way to wake us up and to comfort us.

So, Emma has taken over taking care of us. And showing us that she loves us. And showing us that she, like Natty, is a little bit human. And she expects the best. And she is regal and elegant. We realized, she is our new princess. And then we knew... Emma is the new Natty.

Decide to Let Go

haven't talked a lot about the decision to end Natty's life… at least not the struggle of it all. For one, I loathe having that kind of influence over another living being. To make the decision of life or death… And yet, dying with dignity is a real thing. I want to die with dignity. Which means someone will have to make that decision about me. But it will be someone I empower to make that decision. Someone I choose. Someone I tell that I do not want extraordinary efforts to be made. I get to make that decision. But, to make that decision without her input…

I almost did not even write this story, but then I had sign after sign that this story is necessary. I literally have had four friends in as many months tell me about making the end of life decision for their puppy. It is heartbreaking. And I see the pain on everyone's face, hear it in their voice and feel the anguish in their heart. It is one of the worst decisions any pet parent will have to make.

When it came to Natty, by the time we discovered the cancer in her spine, we already knew that she had an enlarged heart and her kidneys were weak. So, surgery was more than risky. We had a 40% chance of a successful surgery. But add the complication of medications further weakening her kidneys. And add that the surgery could further weaken her heart, we made the tough decision that it was best to let her live out her days. Without surgery we were given three to six months. We would have done anything for Natty. Absolutely anything. But now, what could we do but nothing? How could we do nothing? The decision to do nothing… to just let her live out her remaining days… it seemed kind and cruel all at once. But I anchored to it being easier for her.

After all, I had the experience with Ashley. I did everything to keep her alive. Took all risks. Made all the heroic efforts. But the heroics were only on me and my bank account. I had not thought about how hard it would be on her little body. How weak she already was. I just thought my love was enough to give her the will to fight. I was determined not to make the same mistake. I was going to put Natty first. I was going to take every consideration. And money or no, it was kinder to Natty to let her go at her own pace. And this is how I convinced myself I was being kind to her.

In reality, there is a point to where we know there is a real possibility that we will outlive our pet. We may not think about it at first, but eventually, we see the signs of age. Our baby may lose her hearing, or his sight. He may develop some disease – be it cancer, arthritis, seizures, or something else that is untreatable or inoperable. Or maybe we just see the signs of aging as they start to grey or slow down. It is that point in time that is the most gut wrenching. Mostly because it does not happen all at once; the realization is so slow until one day, it hits you like a ton of bricks. You say their age out loud and you just know… the time is near.

This is what happened with Natty… she never greyed because her coat was the loveliest cream color. But, I saw the signs of her age starting to show. We adopted Dolly so that she would carry forward some bit of Natty. And bringing Dolly brought back some of her youth… until one day when it was undeniable. She was moving less. Her eyes were getting more and more cloudy with cataracts. And she was losing her hearing. Even worse, she was having more accidents. We knew… it was nearing her time. But it was easy to ignore. She acted so well… and relied so heavily on Dolly that it was hard to tell. But… it was happening. What signs do you see? Which ones should we ignore?

A friend recently lost her Chihuahua. I wasn't there, but I heard the story and it broke my heart knowing exactly what she was going through. Apparently, a few days earlier, the thought had crossed her mind that she will not have another season with her baby. It was a fleeting thought really. Just a general acknowledgment that his time was nearing. Fast forward two days - it was a normal day... she was hanging out with a friend... they were doing chores around the house. The pup wanted to cling to her. But since she was working with power tools and did not want him to get hurt, she put him inside. They were taking a break and out of nowhere, he started to cry and whimper. She swooped him up and started to comfort him. She told him she loved him, and then just like that, he was gone. Without any notice. He was just gone.

Part of me rejoiced for her that she had no decision to make. And part of me ached for her that she had no time to prepare for this emotional tidal wave. With or without warning, losing a fur-baby is like a full tsunami. They have full blown personalities. We have full relationships with them. Our love for them is real. And their love for us is real. I cannot begin to imagine what my friend went through on that day. One day she decided to do her chores... one day, she put her baby in the house to protect him from the power tools outside. One day he cried and passed from this earth. I sit here and try to write about her experience. But all I feel is the great chasm of shock and emptiness. And then I think to my own experience... the day we put Natty down... I felt the same thing: shock and emptiness. And yet, I knew. I had more than fair warning.

Lessons Learned from My Rescue Dog

I guess it doesn't matter. Death of a loved one is death. Loss is loss. All that is left is the hole in our hearts. And the sweet memories of their antics. And the love. The love carries us. That love helps us move on. That love encourages us to adopt again.

The Spirit Lives On

Today, my friend Brian had to put down his dog. He has had her since she was a puppy and now she is sixteen. Today is also the Monday after the Thanksgiving holiday which means that he spent the entire four days either at the vet or nursing her at home. When I saw the email from him, I actually felt happy for the pup and relieved for him and his family. After all, it sounded like they all knew she was transitioning and it was the end of her suffering. And yet, I know how much he and his whole family would miss her. I felt stuck. I tried to think back to how I felt when Natty transitioned. I remember the feeling of relief when Glenn finally understood it was her time. I remember how sad I felt when I saw her face and there was not a smile, but a pained hollow look of exhaustion. By the time we let her go, her soul had already vacated. And yet, there she was... a sweet soul that brought our family together. She created a family out of tragedy. She found my soul, picked Glenn and Dolly. For the soul that she was, I missed her as we put her down. As the life drained from her body, I cried for the physical presence that would no longer inhabit our home. And yet, I rejoiced for the spiritual freedom we were giving her. In my soul, I felt her gratefulness…. For letting her body go.

We came home and neither Dolly nor Emma seemed to be fazed at her not coming back with us. Could it be that they knew? Could it be that it was just another trip to the vet for them? I will never know. They never showed a sign. In truth, I felt a heaviness in my heart for a few days… and as the weekend passed, so did that heaviness. Did the relief come because we no longer had to carry her up and down the stairs every couple of hours? Did it come from not having to spend so much time prepping food for her? Did it come because we did not have to clean up after her so much? Or did it come because her soul was still with us? Was she present in the love Dolly has for Emma? Or was she in the love we all shared for one another?

Whatever the reason, relief swept the house. A weight seemed to have lifted. We marveled at how little clean up we had, and how easy food time was. And yet… there was a quiet to the house. A vast hollow emptiness. She was six pounds. None of our animals are vocal, and yet, suddenly, there was too much quiet. There was a void. A deep empty echo. She was missed. All at once, I could see her in every corner of the house, in every soul that inhabited the home, and yet, she was nowhere. All of this echoing abyss plus relief reverberated in my soul. How could it be both?

And then I realized, she will always be here. She will be in everything I do. And she will be in everything I am. I will see her in the hero-worship Dolly has for Emma. I will see her in Dolly's joy on her walks. I will see her in Emma cleaning Georgie. I will see her in the Facebook memories. Once a while, I will even see her sleeping on the bed, or in the sunshine… I will see her in everything. All this, and I still cannot feel sorry that she is gone. I am actually relieved for her. Glad for her transition. She was ready to go. And yet, she will never truly be gone.

So, what do I say to Brian? "Thank goodness you did not have to do this for longer than four days?" Or, "I am glad she did not suffer for longer?" Or, "She will never really be gone." Anything I say sounds trite, even to me.

So… what can I say? My dear Brian, she is still there. She will never really be gone. I am happy you had so much lovely time with her. I am glad she did not suffer too much or too long. I am certain her soul will be with you forever more. I am certain she is one of the many angels you can access at any given time. I am certain you will miss her presence. But if you listen, you will hear her. And if you unfocus your eyes just enough or look in your dreams, you will see her wagging her tail, doing your favorite trick, and sitting right there by your side.

With love from Natalie.

Acknowledgements

This book was conceived at a fantastic party hosted by TUT in Santa Fe where we dreamed of infinite possibilities and were encouraged to imagine our future selves. Many people helped and encouraged me in the writing, and I'd like to take this opportunity to thank them.

To my husband Glenn for his amazing love and support through this project and all my life, and for loving Natty immediately.

For Brian, Britten, and Franki, who each inspired one of the stories.

To Cinnamon for fostering Natty and countless other puppies and always caring about the animal world. She works with www.savingk9livesplus.org/

To the Atlanta Humane Society for all of their work helping animals, and for helping me rescue Emma and Georgie.

To Kaari for her help in formulating this idea and bringing it into reality, and her continued support in editing and encouraging me – always.

To Mike Dooley, without whom I never would have thought to take my first baby step as an author and write the first story, then continue on to take all the next steps that became this book. His work has been a guiding force and inspiration for many people, including myself. www.tut.com

To NOAH, for rescuing Dolly and fostering her until we could bring her home. www.thenoahcenter.org

To A. Rose for the lovely portrait of Natalie that graces this book's cover. You can find more of her work at her instagram account bloomingpurplerose.

To Anni Kemp for being the love lady. Annikemp.com

And last but definitely not least, to Tara for being my Max. And for being the best big sister to Natty. 17.

About the Author

Mollie Singh is a college professor, writer, Infinite Possibilities trainer, and IT Program Manager. She grew up in Los Angeles, where she wrote her first book, an Indian cook book. She later moved to Seattle, where she adopted Natalie and Dolly and met her husband Glenn. She attended California State University, Northridge, and holds an MBA from Georgia Institute of Technology. She volunteers her time with Second Helpings Atlanta and the ACLU.

She and her husband live in Atlanta where they adopted Emma and Georgie.

If your nonprofit animal organization would like copies of this book for fundraising or similar events, please contact the author at molliesingh@yahoo.com.

www.molliesingh.com

51105159R00088

Made in the USA
Columbia, SC
13 February 2019